T0131504

AN ENLIGHTENINGLY NEW PATH TO
SUCCESS & GENUINE HAPPINESS

MIND SET, GO!

Think It ... Love It ... Live It

DEBORAH JOHNSON
KENDRA JOHNSON

BALBOA.
PRESS
A DIVISION OF HAY HOUSE

Balboa Press books may be ordered through booksellers or by contacting:

Balboa Press
A Division of Hay House
1663 Liberty Drive
Bloomington, IN 47403
www.balboapress.com
1 (877) 407-4847

Author photo provided by Women With Vision

Print information available on the last page.

ISBN: 978-1-5043-4790-7 (sc)
ISBN: 978-1-5043-4791-4 (e)

Balboa Press rev. date: 2/8/2016

CONTENTS

Acknowledgements

I would like to thank my husband Stanley for all of his years of patience, understanding, love, support and encouragement in all I do. I would like to say thank you to my daughter and co-author Kendra. Over the years Kendra has repeatedly and unintentionally given me insight, wisdom well beyond her years, and a deeper clarity and awareness of a unique mindset. Her ensuing success because of this way of thinking is an inspiration and what will be shared here.

I would also like to thank Bill and Mina Volencz for their inspiration and words of wisdom.

"Deborah, your message is to educate, to let people know they are empowered, always were and always will have the ability to lead their lives with no need for approval. Perception is only a belief, it is not real. We are individuals, we are unique; no two people perceive life the same way.

And that is why I love and respect what you do, bringing awareness to the masses and the message is "don't resist your natural self, act upon your highest excitement, you are unique, challenge your limits and do what you love to do".

Mina Volencz, Educator

MIND SET, GO!

Think It…Love It…Live It
An Enlighteningly New & Easier Path to
Success & Genuine Happiness

INTRODUCTION

(A PAGE FROM MY DAUGHTER'S BOOK)

In so many ways we have become the lost society; the world has become so complex we struggle to grasp our own reality. We try to 'find' ourselves, 'understand' ourselves, 'create' ourselves; or sometimes 'lose' ourselves and shadow another in an attempt to feel fulfilled. What ever happened to simply 'being ourselves'? We question our contentedness and if we are content does that mean we are deceiving ourselves.

Plainly put, we are what and who we are at this point in time. If we are incongruent in ourselves, we are the only ones who can alter those dynamics. We have the ability to live a mentally and emotionally balanced life if we adjust our mindset and follow through with the necessary actions to create it.

If we trust in our own beliefs, our thoughts, our values and our individual traits we will attract those who resonate with us. If we veer away from our natural characteristics and qualities to accommodate anything or anyone else, we will struggle until we 'find' ourselves and put ourselves back on our personal track again.

This does not mean we only think about ourselves with disregard for others. It does not mean having a rigid, unbending mindset.

The congruence I am talking about is that deep-rooted core belief of what works for us and what does not. If we consistently resonate with ourselves and follow what is in our heart and head, we will never steer ourselves wrong. In fact, you may be pleasantly surprised at those around you who suddenly become more accommodating. You will also find though, some who distance themselves from you as you no longer seem to be on the same wavelength.

Since her childhood, I have watched in fascination as our daughter has unconsciously applied this mindset and concepts to achieve her goals. She has held true to herself, determines and embraces what works for her and discards what does not.

Our daughter has, many times over, given me awareness and understanding that defies her years on this plane. Her ideals are concise; she defines what she wants, sometimes vaguely, sometimes specifically, and then allows the appropriate opportunities to present themselves. Most importantly, she follows through regardless of how her 'want' presents itself.

In Grade 5 our daughter announced she wanted to do a French Exchange in Grade 8, which was the earliest age any student exchanges were offered. My husband assured her he would consider her going to Quebec. She emphatically stated that by French exchange she meant France. Quebec was not an option. In Grade 8 our daughter went to France for 3 months.

In Grade 9 our daughter then announced she wanted to do another exchange, but this time to Costa Rica. In Grade 10 off she went. She wanted to take Grade 12 biology in the Costa Rican rainforest. That summer she headed to Costa Rica for a condensed 4-week summer program to acquire her biology credit before entering Grade 12.

Every step of the way the finances presented themselves, in some way either through us, or as she got older through her own means, for her to achieve these goals.

Now an adult, she still follows the same basic mindset she exercised in her earlier years. She wants it in her heart, envisions it in her mind and takes action to make it reality.

Like the rest of us, Kendra has her highs and lows, fears and anxieties, trials and tribulations. However what I have witnessed time and again is that she is very quick to recognize when she is out of sync with herself and she opens up to whatever opportunity comes to correct this. This action is what maintains congruency.

Kendra may not know what her exact steps will be, she knows the end result she wants and allows God, Universe, Powers That Be to lay the stepping stones of opportunity out for her. This is where listening to that inner voice, trust in receiving what you have asked for and then acting upon it comes into play. To say it again, if we follow this simple mindset to orchestrate and direct our intentions, synchronicity will always work in conjunction with our intentions.

As mentioned earlier our daughter is not perfect nor is the following meant to idolize her. Rather, to give an understanding of how she integrates congruency in self, synchronicity of a higher energy, and the process of thinking and willing to create her physical reality.

It is these observations and defining this mindset that is put forth in the following pages. In addition to referencing Kendra also included are stories of others I have connected with through the years who I have seen instinctively exercising the same mindset to live their lives and achieve their goals successfully (by their benchmark). Simplistic in concept as one tiers naturally into the next, once fully understood and implemented, one can begin to embrace the contentedness of life to the fullest.

Mindset

Six Steps to Success & Genuine Happiness

1. **GENEROSITY**
   Be considerate, caring & generous to those around you, but not to a fault.

2. **BALANCE**
   Be selfish – learn to say NO. Finding the perfect balance between your needs and helping others will create overall happiness. You can't make someone else happy until you are happy yourself.

3. **INDIVIDUALITY**
   No matter how popular, funny or amazing you think someone else is, they possess faults that you do not, many of which you may not know about. Everyone has their own strengths and weaknesses, embrace both and see how to improve upon your weaknesses. Don't BE someone else.

4. **GOAL & VISION**
   Commit to it and be prepared to act on it immediately. Outline what you want, know that is what you want, picture yourself already in that situation. It will come quickly so be prepared....

5. RIPPLE EFFECT AND SYNCHRONICITY

Trust that the 'ripple effect' of your choices & decisions will ultimately result in better for all – if it doesn't come to fruition, then it wasn't in the best interest for everyone.

6. YOUR WORLD

Don't make someone else your world and don't allow someone to make you their world – be PART of their world and let them be PART of yours.

STEP 1

GENEROSITY
(Be considerate, caring & generous to those around you, but not to a fault)

Generosity comes in many forms; monetary is what most think of first but generosity is so much more - caring and consideration in how we think of and treat others; motivating, inspiring, supporting and encouraging others as they walk their personal path. Embracing differences rather than shunning them and allowing others to be themselves without judgment.

True generosity and caring comes from the heart without expectation.

Our daughter has always displayed this generosity unselfishly yet still keeping a balance for herself.

She is the first to help a friend if they need a place to stay. She is selectively generous financially and will be the first to reach into her pocket to help another.

Recently my daughter and I were at the checkout of a large store. The woman in front of us was buying back to school clothing and supplies for her children and seemed quite stressed as she watched the dollars mount up on the cash register. Her young son tugged at her arm and asked if he could go for a ride on the mechanical horse by the entrance. Harried, his mother explained she had no change for the two-dollar ride but it was apparent she wished she could allow her son this small joy.

Without hesitation, my daughter reached into her pocket and handed the woman two dollars, which would allow her son to ride

3

the horse. The woman was dumb-founded and sputtered about paying my daughter back. My daughter simply smiled.

Her gestures are not always financial. If a friend is between residences she will offer short-term accommodation to help out. Although she expects nothing in return she is always rewarded in some form for her consideration and generosity.

Sometimes it is the smallest or simplest act of consideration and generosity that reaps the biggest rewards for both the giver and receiver. If you seek recognition and glory for your deed you will tip the scales negatively as rather than your act being selfless, you have made the gesture selfish, all about you.

When I commented to my daughter about her spontaneous act of kindness she simply shrugged and said "why wouldn't I." Selfless acts of consideration and kindness also come with humbleness and personal gratification – that warm and fuzzy feeling we all love to experience.

The most natural and easy acts of generosity come in the form of praise from one to another. Think about how amazing you feel when someone compliments you for something you do, say or even wear. A simple genuine compliment makes us stand a little straighter. We walk with a little more confidence. Whether we realize we are doing it or not, we smile and those who see it consciously or unconsciously automatically smile in return. A smile is the best form of 'contagious' there is.

The impact praise has on a child is immeasurably positive. The opposite holds true. If praise is consistently lacking then mental, emotional and even physical damage can result as the following story shows.

Whenever a young child of three spoke, or asked if she could say something at mealtime, her father would laughingly reply;

"you're a girl, nobody's interested in what you have to say"

or

"go ahead but I'm sure it won't be intelligent",

or

"what could you possibly say that we would want to hear."

Her older brother would laugh; her mother would quietly reassure her as she fell silent.

Those times when she did speak, her father would comment "that was a silly thing to say", or "clearly your brother got all the brains", or would simply start speaking over her before she finished, drowning her out completely.

Although these statements were meant (for the most part) in jest, they were repeated constantly.

By the age of four this child was withdrawn, seldom spoke anywhere and had developed a speech impediment when she did speak. There was no physical cause for the impediment, which had not been evident in her first three years of life but had developed rapidly as she progressed into her fourth year.

Fortunately a speech pathologist worked successfully with this young child prior to her going into kindergarten, sparing her possible taunting, teasing and further speech deterioration.

Generally, children process the words they hear verbatim. Heard often enough, just as drops of water wear away at a stone, lack of praise, or worse yet, derogatory comments, erode self-confidence significantly. For this young girl it caused a psychologically-based physical limitation.

In this young child's case, her father's sisters were subjected to the same verbal 'humour' at mealtime during his childhood while his mother sat quietly. Now an adult, this father was re-enacting his fathers' commentary, and just as his mother pacified his sisters, his wife now discreetly pacified his daughter. Interesting that this verbal 'bantering' was never directed at the sons, only the daughters.

Generously giving a child praise and positive re-enforcement will allow them to flourish as they feel comfortable stretching the boundaries of their abilities to the maximum.

****

Adults are more inhibited and often not aware of their own attributes until someone points their qualities out to them. Generosity can also come in the form of giving newfound awareness and esteem.

Such was the case of a recently divorced forty-seven year old woman. The only job her husband 'allowed' her to have during their marriage was working with teens at a fast food outlet.

Now on her own she found the pay wasn't adequate and the physical demands for someone her age were becoming excessive. Although she knew retirement wasn't in her cards at this point in her life, she longed for an office job but believed she had no qualifications.

Slumped in her chair across from me, she felt resigned to remain at her current position. However skills are skills and can easily be transferred to fit a new role. Take distribution as an example. It doesn't matter if you're shipping apples or elephants, the basic process of distribution itself is the same, only the packaging is different. All she needed to do was recognize and 'repackage' her skills to meet a new format.

I helped her redefine her skills: "You have strong customer service skills since you deal with customers every day right?" She nodded. "You organize the crews for their shifts so you have organizational skills." She sat up slightly straighter. "It is often excessively busy so you work well under pressure." "I do," she stated with strength and conviction in her voice. "You handle many different tasks at once so you have the ability to multi-task." She began to smile. I continued. "You have no direct supervision so you are a self-starter and self-motivated. You work without instruction or supervision." She was now sitting up poker straight in her chair. "I most certainly do," she replied emphatically. "Lastly, you're team oriented, punctual and reliable."

"Yes I am", she stated matter-of-factly.

"Now take those skills put your resume together and apply for the office job." I said softly.

This previously demoralized woman landed her first office position three weeks later. She was ecstatic.

We all have skills, abilities, gifts and talents we are often unaware of until someone points them out to us. Be generous with your praise.

****

Giving and generosity always brings a balance of Yin and Yang in some form. I recently listened to two middle-aged sisters bantering back and forth about an upcoming fund raiser. One sister emphatically stated how she was giving countless hours to organizing this function and was extremely annoyed at her non-participatory sister. Her sister retorted that her life was so hectic she had no free time to give hence she would be donating with a financial contribution. The first sister countered by explaining curtly how her budget was incredibly tight so giving monetarily was not an option to her. They drew me into their conversation by asking what I thought.

I pointed out that without volunteers to organize and run the function, there wouldn't be a function. The volunteering sister smugly crossed her arms over her chest. I continued by saying that although much was being generously donated for the event, there were still many expenses in the setup that were being covered through financial infusion from those like the other sister. Raising funds for their cause was also the primary reason for the event. The other sister now gloated. I expressed that each sister was contributing equally in their own way; one of her time and other of her money. Both volunteer time and financial support were necessary for overall success. Without one, there wouldn't be the other. They were equal in generosity yet opposite in deliverance.

****

Remember positive attracts positive. Make a conscious effort to reach out with some form of unconditional kindness, consideration and generosity every day even with a few simple words. You will notice significant differences in how much more positively your own life will begin to flow.

For a brief second beforehand think before you speak or act. Think of yourself on the receiving end of all you do. How would your words or actions make you feel if you were the recipient? What if through generosity of giving of yourself in some form, you could make a difference in the lives of those around you? It is an awesome power to wield. Yet we are unaware of it as we seldom if ever think in these terms.

STEP 2

BALANCE

Be selfish – learn to say NO. Finding the perfect balance between your needs and helping others will create overall happiness. You can't make someone else happy until you are happy yourself.

We are conditioned whether consciously or unconsciously to believe that we have to rely on others to make us happy. Children look to their parents to make them happy, and parents constantly strive to appease their children through both monetary and emotional means.

We live in this paradigm where finding that 'right' person and acquiring that 'perfect career' are the only ingredients to a truly happy existence. We count on outside influences to fulfill us. We believe without these there is a gaping void in our lives that we yearn for and frantically seek to fulfill. It is even taught throughout school via past philosophers such as Maslow that we cannot attain our most fulfilling need of self-actualization until we have achieved acceptance and increased self-esteem from others.

While there is validity to the hierarchy, what if we ignored it and adopted the opposite mindset of general contentedness with ourselves here and now? Would we eliminate this need for 'perfection'? Would the rest of the hierarchy fall into place for us – esteem and love and belonging? What if we suddenly realized that we are solely responsible for our happiness?

We have all experienced being in the presence of someone who, simply through their sheer positive energy and vibrancy inspires us and motivates us – makes us feel like the best versions of ourselves.

We have also all experienced the opposite by interacting with someone who very quickly leaves us feeling drained, despondent and unhappy.

Just as others affect us, we too affect those around us through our words, actions and moods. It is not our nature to always be happy and positive; everyone's emotional pendulum's swing to different degrees, with varying highs and lows. It's called life. However if we focus on what we emit rather than what we receive, we will quickly come to realize that 'giving is in actuality receiving'. When we share our positive energy with others, we receive it back ten-fold through their reaction to us. This awareness and conscious effort is the foundation for balance in our lives.

Unconditional contentedness comes from within and radiates outward. It does not come from outside in, as we are taught. It comes from you being settled and happy with who you are, where you're at, and what you have at this particular stage of your life. The measuring stick should be by your benchmark and no one else's.

Unfortunately, we are conditioned to believe that by putting ourselves first we are selfish and inconsiderate. It is this thinking that has segregated our race into givers and takers. What does it take to attain this balance between give and receive? Learn to say 'no'. If giving to someone or something is unconditional and makes you feel happy, then keep on giving. However if your giving is driven by someone else's needs or wants and this instance makes you angry, resentful, hurt or frustrated, simply say 'no'.

You may say 'well, who else will do it', or 'it's expected of me', or 'I've always done it so I can't stop now'. Of course you can. One of two things will happen when you say 'no'. Either, the person will begin doing more for themselves, or they will find someone else to do their bidding for them.

They will always make sure you know they found someone else to meet their needs, making you feel guilty for finally saying 'no'. Although for a brief second you certainly may feel a pang of guilt, this will quickly shift to an amazing sense of relief and freedom by lifting an unwanted burden from your life.

Simple Philosophy:

If you genuinely love doing something or helping someone continue to do so. If you're upset or frustrated just say 'no I'm sorry I can't'.

Remember, there needs to be balance of give and take - you don't have to justify to anyone why you choose to do or not do something. Hold true to what works for you and what doesn't.

Our daughter always believes by maintaining balance in your own life you are contributing to proper balance in those around you; sometimes directly, sometimes indirectly. The choices you make may not thrill others initially, but when all is said and done they too will usually be better off and thankful.

Focus only on balancing your life. Others will align accordingly for everyone's highest good. Do not feel it is your job to balance the lives of others; they arrived on their own, will depart on their own and need to create the balance the works for them alone.

Think of your life as a choir. It takes the blending of many different voices to create the final unified sound of a choir. Tenors sing together, sopranos sing together, altos sing together and so on. By putting voices with like voices they compliment and support each other. If however you were to mix the different vocals up so a tenor was next to a soprano, who was next to an alto, then asked them to sing, the result would be musical torture to the ears.

All members of the choir may enjoy singing together but when each member is placed with those they most closely harmonize with, sheer musical magic results.

Life is just like the choir. You will always find there are those in your life you 'harmonize' with and those that may 'strike the wrong cord'. Through respect and appreciation of others' individual tones, we can all stand together to produce an amazing 'choir', but choose to surround yourself most closely to those in natural harmony with you.

Above all else, hold true to yourself first and foremost. The word 'no' was put into our vocabulary for a reason. Use it when appropriate for you.

Many years ago I worked with an incredibly dynamic woman with two children who was in the process of starting over and rebuilding her life. When her children were just toddlers her extremely well educated husband walked away from a wonderful position. The company was restructuring. He didn't want the possible humiliation of being let go, hence he simply quit. He used the excuse that their children needed a parent versus daycare and so remained unemployed for the next eleven years. During this time his wife, now the sole income earner, built up a very successful business with three busy offices, purchased land, and built the house of her dreams for her and her family.

Although his unemployment was a constant argument between them throughout those years, he refused to return to work.

Finally, she said "No. No more". She filed for divorce and although it cost her the home she loved (he got to keep the house for the sake of the children) and destroyed her business (he got half), she had her freedom to live her life unencumbered by another.

Within two weeks of final settlement and payout her ex-husband landed an incredibly well paying full-time job ($150,000 annually) in his former field. As he was no longer being supported by his wife, or needed the excuse of his children to remain unemployed, he gave her sole custody. He walked away from all responsibility while profiting handsomely.

Undaunted, she set about building a new business and putting herself in a financial position to move out of the tiny two bedroom apartment she now shared with her children.

Interestingly, she rebuilt herself in an amazingly short period of time. She met a wonderful (and coincidentally extremely wealthy man) who she ended up very happily married to.

Had she not had the courage and conviction to say 'no', she would still be in an unhappy marriage and working excessive hours to involuntarily support another who refused to do for himself.

****

Saying 'no' when applicable not only defines you and holds self-respect intact, it also forces definition of those you have said 'no' to, as they must then redefine themselves in some way to accommodate the change. Action will always create reaction of some form and if the intent of the action is positive, the reactions will also be positive overall.

STEP 3

INDIVIDUALITY

Hold true to yourself and your beliefs. No matter how popular, or funny or amazing you think that other person is, they possess faults that you do not. Everyone has their own triumphs and struggles; embrace both and see how to improve upon your weaknesses for you. Don't BE someone else.

As proud parents we all remember times when our children made choices whether it was through what they did, said, or wore, that made them stand out from others. Some love to conform and blend in with their peers while others choose to express their individuality.

When she was very young, our daughter would often wear two different coloured socks and would assure us she had another pair exactly like them in her drawer. It was just what motivated her that day as she was dressing.

Like her socks, her choices were never outlandish, extreme or attention grabbing, just subtly different. In every instance our daughter would come home a day or two later complaining that others in the class were now doing the same thing – different coloured socks, a new way of wearing an outfit or changing their hair, just as she had a few days prior. We used to tell her that 'copying was the highest form of flattery' to which she would always reply, 'but now everyone is just like me, not like them.' At the ripe age of six, she was on to something. Why does everyone strive to be someone else, when they are much more interesting as themselves?

Our daughter's unique heritage helped to fuel some of her individuality. She is a Mulatto - a mix of Coloured with her father being half Coloured/half Caucasian, and Caucasian on my side. When she was four years old she came home from junior kindergarten one day and told us there was a really nice new little girl in her class who was black. We asked her why she would use those words to describe her classmate. She frowned at our question then innocently, matter of factly replied 'because *that is* the colour she is'.

We explained to her that she also has some colour in her. She is part Coloured and part White. We made the error of using the word 'part' in describing this to our young babe, and she naively responded with "but which part?" while examining her appendages as if a third, different-coloured arm were going to appear out of thin air. How refreshing innocence is!

She has always been extremely proud of this lineage. Interestingly enough, she has been taken for Spanish, Mexican, Indian, African American and Portuguese. Her appearance and personality allows her to often blend seamlessly with a multitude of backgrounds and being a people person and traveler, she thrives on using this trait. Her friends have lovingly dubbed her as 'The Ethnic Chameleon.'

Every person, regardless of age, race, religion or beliefs, is unique unto themselves. Expressing our true selves to others is what also defines our circle of influence and associated experiences.

Unfortunately, our society, marketing and media set unrealistic perfection-based benchmarks that most consciously or unconsciously follow to be accepted.

Our youth is constantly bombarded with contradictory messages from 'be a team player, get along with everyone, fit in' to 'be unique, be yourself, don't follow the crowd'. This causes inner conflict and in order to accommodate this conflict many resort to emulating another they view as more successful, happy or accepted. The fear of rejection or failure often forces individuals to adopt traits that they may not otherwise possess.

Several years ago I spoke with a couple of graduating eighteen year-olds who had been dating throughout high school. In conversation, I mentioned to the young man that he and his girlfriend seemed like a great match for each other. He told me how strongly he felt about her, he hoped to marry her someday. Following this comment, he added that although she had a very nice figure, her hips were too big and she should do something about them. I was shocked at his comment and asked why he thought that, when she clearly had a very trim athletic build.

He replied that she wasn't as slim as a particular model adorning many magazine covers. This was the benchmark this young man had set and had carried into his relationship with a young lady he adored everything [else] about.

Later, his girlfriend confided to me that she was desperately trying to diet and slim down to please him. She had always thought she had a nice trim build and never realized her hips were disproportionate to the rest of her. (She was actually beautifully proportioned!) In her efforts to correct this flaw apparent to her boyfriend, she developed anorexia and ultimately needed treatment to overcome this distorted view of herself. Her warped perception was created in part by her boyfriend's ideals and in part by our media-driven definition of perfection.

She finally came to realize that if someone loves you, they love you for who and what you are. If they need or want to change you to fit their perceptions, they need to move along and find someone who more closely fits their criteria. No one has the right to change another nor should anyone significantly change themselves to accommodate another person or relationship.

Hold true solely to whom you are and you will attract those who rightfully belong around you.

I worked with a middle-aged woman who expressed that after two failed marriages she finally found total contentment in her third relationship.

She laughingly described how with her first two relationships, she would rise, shower, dress and don her makeup before her spouse even stirred. She 'shadowed' each spouse, making their 'wish list' hers, placing herself in a subservient role to accommodate her partner (which ironically was how she saw her mother interact with her father during her upbringing.) She became the chameleon, moulding and shaping herself to fit the way of life unconsciously established by her partner. Did either husband ask her to do this for them? No. Did she do it as a result of her childhood impressions? Yes.

Incongruent in herself, she couldn't understand why she was still incredibly unhappy in each relationship when she was following the 'cookie-cutter' marriage of her seemingly contented parents. Living a façade, it was no surprise both of her marriages eventually ended in divorce.

After her second divorce and feeling she was the failure, she began soul searching. The result was a determination to hold true to herself, a 'what you see is what you get' attitude. She decided in order to be happy the next person had to fall in love with her; complete with frumpy but comfortable dressing gown, curlers, unbrushed teeth and 'morning breath' until she had enjoyed her two cups of extra-strength coffee. Unless some new person could love and accept her for her – even without makeup, she would remain now-contentedly single.

As fate would have it, she met a wonderful man who fell in love with her, curlers and all. She doesn't put her makeup on until she is ready to, and has been incredibly happily married for the last twelve years.

Had she continued the façade of trying to be what she 'perceived' someone else wanted, she would have attracted the same type of man as in her first two marriages and in all likelihood would be either unhappily married again or going through divorce number three.

****

Every person and every living thing is individual and unique unto themselves – that is why we are called individuals. No one will ever be able to know you and love you for who you are if you keep yourself mentally and emotionally hidden or if you attempt to alter yourself to suit another. Appreciate that not everyone will love you nor will you love them. That is reality. However if you embrace yourself and celebrate all of those little idiosyncrasies that contribute to making you unique, you will be less aware of what you are 'supposed to be' by other standards. You will gain a comfort and contentedness in yourself that you will effortlessly share with others simply by being you.

STEP 4

GOAL & VISION
Set your goal & vision – commit to it and be prepared to act on it immediately. Outline what you want, know that is what you want, picture yourself already in the situation. It will come quickly so be prepared...

Someone once said to me 'separate your dreams from reality, dreams are wonderful but reality pays the bills.'

The truth of the matter is that our dreams not only can be, but also should be our reality. All we have to do is commit to what we want, be prepared to act on it IMMEDIATELY, and learn to take a chance on ourselves.

Far too often we place our own fears and self-doubts foremost, sabotaging ourselves before we even begin the journey. Any journey is worth taking and success comes in many forms along the way. Sometimes these successes are unrecognizable and the silver lining can only be seen in hindsight. It is important to learn to view these masked triumphs in the moment, rather than as an 'A-HA!' much later on.

We also place our fears, apprehensions and doubts on those around us. We do it under the guise of 'wanting what's best for them' or 'wanting to keep them out of harms' way'. In reality we are trying to keep ourselves in our own comfort zone by convincing others to maintain what we consider to be status quo.

Some time back I spoke with a mother who complained that her twenty-year-old son was lying around the house, unmotivated and despondent. She explained that she and her husband had convinced their son to learn a trade (plumber) so he would always have a secure career and financial stability. I asked her if a trade was what he wanted to do. Without a solid yes or no, she then expanded upon her and her husband's reasoning.

Education done and now needing an apprenticeship, her son had only sent out one resume that had been rejected because they did not have openings at the time.

Again, I asked her if the path was her son's choice. Finally she confessed that they had pushed him into it, no it was not his wish. I asked if he had ever mentioned what he wanted to do. "Oh yes," she commented instantly, "he wants to be a Personal Trainer...but that field is so demanding to even get into, the pay isn't good to start and there really isn't any long-term security in it."

"Is your son athletic?" I asked.

"Best in his school," she replied.

"Does he enjoy working with and being around people?"

"Gift of the gab!" she said enthusiastically.

"So...you suggest a non-athletic career...where he works on his own with little people contact... in a field he has absolutely no interest in...and wonder why he is unmotivated and despondent...?"

This was her moment of realization.

I explained that he always had the plumbing trade education to fall back on should his passion not pan out.

"I never looked at it that way, we just wanted what we thought was best for him" she muttered.

I continued gently, "Why don't you and your husband talk, then sit down with your son and tell him you support his goals. I know how much you love him, and want him to be happy and successful. Ask him what he needs to get going with becoming a personal trainer and encourage him to do it."

She called back several months later to say that within days of giving their encouragement her son had secured a full time job at a local gym, was already training with a coach to work one-on-one with clients, and had enrolled in the college course for his newfound field.

She told me she was astounded at the remarkable change in his attitude, energy and enthusiasm. Although the money certainly wasn't that good right now, she was starting to see his earning potential for the future.

She said she felt like she had her son back. Laughing, she also happily stated that the downside of this was she and her husband never got to see their son anymore because he was always at the gym!

Just as we sometimes hold others back, we also rationalize why we can't take THAT opportunity we just asked for. It comes under the guise of 'responsibility' or 'unrealistic'. The reality is that if we change the dynamics of our life, the responsibilities will automatically adjust in accordance to the changes we make.

Here are some of the most common excuses we use:

"I'd love to take that promotion but it would involve a move and the family wouldn't be happy." Do you know that for a fact, had you already asked them how they would feel or are you just assuming for them?

"It would take money I don't think I have right now, so I'll have to pass." When someone truly wants to do something and commits to it, the money also finds its way to you in some form to create your reality.

Several years ago I connected with a woman who excitedly told me of her 'manifesting experience'. She needed to make a business trip to China the following month, didn't have the finances for the trip or means to gain the funds. Believing strongly in 'creating', she put out to the Universe that a way and means of making this trip would manifest itself as long as it was for everyone's highest good. She didn't focus on the need for a ticket, she focused only on the end result she sought. Clearly in her mind, she envisioned herself already in China.

She kept revisiting this one mental image. She acted on her need by calling airlines, checking seat sales, etc. and rather than fret and worry, she calmly trusted the opportunity would present itself as necessary. She would jump at the opportunity when it did arise; no matter what form it came in.

Thirty-six hours later she received a phone call from a friend whose travel companion was unable to make a trip the following month. Rather than forfeit the non-refundable seat her companion was prepared to give her ticket to another for free rather than have it go to waste. Remote as the chances were, the trip was to China. Did my client know anyone who might want to use the ticket? She held her breath as she asked about the travel dates. Coincidentally enough, the dates coincided exactly with the dates she needed. Synchronicity is a wonderful thing!

She sent a silent 'thank you' upwards as she excitedly accepted the offer.

Unexpectedly my client reimbursed the woman one-half of the ticket price six months later when she had the money. The woman eagerly accepted as her car had broken down only the day before and she didn't have funds for the repairs. The repayment was exactly the amount she required. Once again, synchronicity came into play.

Unbeknownst to her, this woman used the same mindset that I have watched my daughter use successfully over the years. Keep your mind free of worry and clutter. Keep your goal singular. Set your sights on only one objective at a time and maintain only that line of sight and end result until it is achieved. Initiate some form of action into it (a phone call, conversation, inquiry…), something to generate motivational energy around it. Imagine already living it as if it is your present reality. When the opportunity comes in whatever fashion, move past your fears and embrace it as long as it allows you to hold true to yourself. If it comes in the form of 'stepping stones' toward the goal, mentally move that little foot forward in the new direction you have been asking for. Take those first steps. More will appear to accommodate you.

If you put out numerous wishes and goals simultaneously you will splay your energies into too many directions and your results will be scattered, fragmented and most likely unfulfilled.

You can't make it to the end of the path if you don't start walking along it. Standing in one spot both mentally and emotionally (and sometimes physically in the literal sense) is only going to give you one result…you will forever find yourself standing in that one spot.

I would like you to think of the following two scenarios in relation to no right or wrong path in life, only linking experiences that help define us.

A young man desperately seeking a change from his current dead-end job saw a 'clerk wanted' sign in a store window. He entered, applied with the store manager and was hired instantly.

He found he had such an affinity to the product line he was selling he enrolled himself in university to learn about the process of making this particular product and upon graduation landed a position in the manufacturing end of this industry.

His passion for it advanced him very quickly and within a short time he was responsible for overseeing all processing for his company. He has also been fortunate enough to travel abroad through his firm to share his extensive knowledge with those in underprivilaged countries entering the industry.

His original thought and need was only to gain a job as a clerk in a store. Unaware at that time of how this would manifest into so much more, his amazing career evolved from this one action of simply inquiring.

The second scenario involves a young woman who started along her original career path by obtaining her BA in Psychology. Needing to work for a year afterward to fund her Masters Degree she came to realize she wanted to change her career to Nursing.

Hence, rather than paying for her Masters she immersed herself in a field that at the time seemed to her friends and family unrelated to her first degree. She later stated though while working for that one year she came to realize what she really wanted to do with her life was be a nurse in a psychiatric ward or psychiatric hospital, which required education in both fields.

Although all she sought originally was her Psychology Degree, as her life progressed she successfully blended one path with another to create her final career which she is passionate about.

Most importantly of all, in everything you do, choose what excites, inspires and motivates you. Or for the very least, find something that interests you to the point as though you could do it happily for many years if it were to evolve and see where it leads you. The money and success will grow with it.

Where others are concerned, allow them to dream their dreams, strive for their goals, and support them with the path they choose to walk. Don't allow your fears to hold you or those around you back.

Every time my daughter has 'sent out' a wish she has acted on the result. We have choices to hold with what is familiar or delve headlong into what is new. Life truly is nothing more than a series of choices when you think about it. If we pass up on that opportunity when we have asked for it, we may wait a long time for the next one to present itself.

I dealt with a woman who wanted to move into a computer-based position but had no related experience or skills and no excess funds for school. I told her a friend of hers would offer to train her for free in her off-hours. The training would give her the skills she would need for an upcoming job in this friends' company and the friend would also recommend her for the position. However it was imperative she take the free training when offered.

A year later this same woman contacted me, complaining because the path I had described to her had not materialized.

I asked her if a friend had offered to give her free computer training. She stated that yes that offer had been made but she passed on it because it was winter time and she didn't like going out at night in the cold and snow.

I then asked her if a job had come available in her friends' company. She explained that about four months after declining the training a position had indeed come up.

"Did you apply for it," I queried.

"Well no I didn't. How could I when I didn't have the necessary skills," she snapped.

So, if you had taken the free training – from someone who was willing to help you – and teach you in her own spare time – you could have applied for that job because you would have been qualified?"

There was a long pause.

"Yes I could have," she finally replied.

I asked if there was any chance this friend was still willing to teach her.

"Unfortunately not, she now lives in another province. Except for night school, which I can't afford, I have no way of gaining the knowledge I need. Besides, since night school runs through the winter months I would still have to be out in the cold at night instead of home with my family so that wouldn't work anyway."

She had already defined her priorities which would always limit her.

To this day this woman still longs for that computer-based job. No matter how hard she thinks or dreams about it the opportunities will continue to slide by unless she takes those necessary educational steps first. The opportunity of 'the steps' to achieve her dream had been given to her. She chose to not take them.

After one of my speaking engagements a man in his late twenties came up and spoke with me. He thanked me for clarifying in my presentation, some of the dynamics from his childhood that had held him back for years.

My information gave him such insight into himself and his family, he felt compelled to share his thoughts with me. Since his early teens he had dreamed of becoming a police officer. His family continuously assured him he did not have what it takes to be a policeman and suggested a number of alternative jobs they felt he would be better suited to.

He explained further that throughout his childhood, any goals he may have had in all areas of his life were always quickly dashed by his father, his mother, or both. By the time he reached adulthood he felt he wasn't particularly capable of doing anything and what he did achieve was met with criticism and judgment. Throughout all this he still always envisioned himself as a police officer and could not imagine himself as anything else. Too afraid of failing though, he had never pursued it.

However, as this young man talked to me about following his dream I watched him become animated and excited about his future. I asked him what he planned to do with this long sought after dream and newfound inspiration.

He assured me he would be applying to the Police Academy and any additional courses necessary to ensure he was accepted. He was going to be a police officer.

Many months passed before I heard from him again. He sent me notification of his pending graduation from the Police Academy which he graduated from at the top of his class.

The last time I heard from this young man he had already moved up through the ranks quickly, was seeking and was most likely to receive a promotion to Detective.

As for his negative family, they proudly boasted that they had suggested and supported their son in becoming a policeman. He never bothered trying to correct them. He had followed his heart and achieved his dream. For him that was all that mattered.

Not all decisions in our lives are in our control. Sometimes fate steps in and plays a role. A single unattached thirty-three year old woman was repositioned and relocated when her company restructured and moved their offices to the other side of the country. As openings in her field were scarce and as furious as she was about the decision, she felt she had no option but to move with them.

She found once she settled in though she absolutely loved her new location, home and position. Where she had no advancement opportunities with her past job, this new role had a multitude of areas she could grow into.

Within months of relocating she also met a well-established man several years her senior and they married the following year. Although they were not changes she initiated or an opportunity she sought, she accepted the path that opened up to her and has never looked back with regret.

....

Where your goals are concerned, you can close your eyes and wish and dream all you want. You can create vision boards or jot down notes on what you are going to do and review that list every day but the bottom line is nothing will ever happen without you putting action to it. The slightest, simplest action from talking with someone about your goals, making a phone call, sending an note, text or email, anything that has an action to it and 'puts your goal out there' will energetically start the process of reaction.

This action/reaction process is what drives the creation of our upcoming reality. If you do nothing, that in itself will create your reality which will be nothing. Your life will go on as it is. If you want change you have to initiate it. Step past your fears and limitations. Treat your goals as adventures to be embarked upon. Embrace the opportunities that will come quickly, and boldly step forward into what you just asked for.

STEP 5

'RIPPLE EFFECT' CONGRUENCY & SYNCHRONICITY
*Every decision and choice you make causes a 'ripple effect.'
When making these decisions, trust that the outcomes from
these ripples will ultimately result in the best for all parties. If
it doesn't come to fruition, then it wasn't in the best interest for
everyone.*

We are the center of our own universe. That is human nature.
We think of our actions, choices and decisions as they affect us
but seldom do we truly think of how our simplest actions ripple
outward to impact those around us.

We are so conditioned to striving, growing, achieving and
succeeding (by often unrealistic benchmarks) that we don't take
the time to realize, we may already have what we think we are
striving for.

Several weeks ago I had a forty-three year old woman ask me if it
was alright to be content with who you are and your life in general?
She wondered if she was missing something or something was
wrong with her. Her family and friends all seemed to be striving
and 'working' so hard toward their goals but never seeming to
reach them.

What was wrong with her? She asked.

Comparing herself to them, she worried that being as content as
she was, she was actually somehow deluding herself. Why wasn't
she 'longing' as everyone else seemed to be.

I asked her if she felt in her heart she was truly content with all
areas of her life. We covered what I lovingly refer to as our 'five

food groups'; family, health, relationships, career and finances; nodding as she addressed each one. She reaffirmed her deep contentedness with all areas of her life. Furthermore, as she addressed each area she felt those she was connected to were also content.

I congratulated her. She wasn't missing a thing; no there was nothing wrong with her; she had actually achieved what everyone else was seeking.

She breathed a deep sigh of relief. "Oh thank God! I thought there was something wrong with me," she exclaimed.

How sad it is that we seem so accustomed to feeling we need more in some way. We question ourselves even when we are truly happy and content. It is ok to be happy and content with your life – just live it and enjoy it!

Contentedness comes in many forms but first and foremost it needs to come from within. Set your benchmark and sights where you want them to be. Move or change them over time if desired but always by your standards alone, no one else's.

Many years ago my husband worked with an eighteen-year-old young man just coming into the workforce. He was hired at entry level picking orders for the distribution area. My husband believed in promoting from within wherever possible and discovered that the one goal and dream this young man had, was to drive one of the company trucks.

My husband told him what licensing and skills he needed for the position, arranged for the company to pay most of this young man's training, which he eagerly sought, and when the next opening for a truck driver came along, he moved this young man into it. He also gave the young man the route he had hoped for, which was to and from Vancouver Island.

By taking action and gaining the skills required for the job this young man fulfilled his dream.

Shortly after taking this new role, my husband asked this young truck driver where he wanted to set his sights next in the company; what did he want to move up to? The young man seemed surprised by my husband's question.

"Oh no, I don't want to move anywhere else in the company, this is my dream come true, it's what I want to be doing." By this point in time this man was now twenty. He had his plan clearly laid out in his mind. He would drive a company truck, buy a house, invest his money, marry, have children and live a wonderfully contented life.

Fifteen years and several moves later for us, my husband and I were visiting out West and as we drove along the Vancouver Island Highway we saw one of his former company's trucks heading toward us.

"Wouldn't it be funny if the driver was still that same kid," my husband mused.

He flashed his lights at the oncoming truck and as we passed each other my husband and this now thirty-five-ish young man recognized each other.

Both pulled over and spent the next ten minutes conversing. My husband asked about the company, and also how he was doing.

"Still happily driving this truck, as you can see," he quipped. "Only difference now is I bought a nice house on some acreage, and I'm happily married with a wife and two little ones at home. Oh, and I got a dog as well," he proudly exclaimed.

As if that wasn't enough, the company had grown to a point where bonuses and shares were offered to all staff so financially he had done exceptionally well. As far as the company was concerned he was an employer's dream; content to come in and just do the job he was being paid to do.

As simple a lifestyle as this may seem to others you couldn't help but envy him for he had acquired and achieved exactly what he needed to make him happy. He was living the life of his dreams.

Contentedness can come with simplicity and it can also come with complexity, accomplishments and achievements. There are those who constantly need to strive. They set their goals high and expect to reach them. They are forever challenging and changing themselves to fit the new criteria they have defined for themselves.

Differing from those who need to fill a void to achieve contentedness, these 'A' type driven individuals thrive on what is new, different and exciting. To them living life is seeking and embracing one change after another. To them this is fulfillment and contentedness of a more complex nature – contentedness nonetheless by their definition.

Whether our dreams are simple or complex, what we emit through our thoughts, words and actions automatically creates a ripple effect with everything we do.

Remember every action has a reaction.

When you set your dreams in motion the other important component to remember is trust; trust that your decisions are the best for you and also for those around you.

The ripple effect to others may be happily welcomed as mentioned. However, if your choices take another out of their comfort zone in some way your ripple effect may be received with anger, resentment and upset.

Hold true to yourself and fully trust your decisions are for the best interest of all, although they may receive negative reactions initially. As events continue to unfold stemming from your choices and decisions, over time others will realize that although initially painful or unsettling, they too are in a better place or situation because of it.

Put a blanket caveat on your wishes that they be fulfilled for everyone's best interest. By doing this you are ensuring that your wishes will come to you in the fashion most beneficial to all. Still hold true to yourself with these decisions and actions, while respecting the potential impact to others.

If your dream does not come to pass as you envision it, either it was not going to be positive for all concerned or something 'better' is waiting in the wings.

'Better' may come immediately or take time to materialize into reality. If the ripple effect is acknowledged and utilized effectively, your ultimate success will be significantly greater than originally envisioned.

The Ripple Effect also comes from 'God', 'Universe', 'Powers that Be', or 'Creator', whatever your particular belief may be. Understanding this energetic component allows you to trust that events and opportunities will occur when and as appropriate for you. They will come to you not just when you feel you are ready, but when the opportunity itself is ready.

We never take this additional variable into account when fulfilling our goals and dreams. Why? Because we believe we are the centre of our own universe. Yet it is a combination of all factors that gives you your desired outcome. All you have to do is start the process by envisioning you are already living your goal *and put action of some form to it.*

What ripples out from us positively as thoughts, ideas, objectives and dreams will ripple back to us in positive form. You cannot dictate or control this form but usually in ripples back as opportunities, contacts, connections and stepping stones that will lead you to your desired outcome – if, and only if you move past your fears and follow that path.

You don't need to focus on 'using' the ripple effect, we emit it with everything that we do – it is our very energy. What we do need to be cognizant of is how we emit this energy to everything around us. We can turn the tide in our favour where our goals and dreams, relationships and overall contentedness is concerned.

I am sure all of us have experienced those occasions when we start our day off feeling wonderfully optimistic and content. We encounter someone who for whatever reason is having 'a bad' day and even if they aren't venting openly, devote much of their time to stomping around, grumbling, huffing and puffing negatively.

Often over a short period of time our mood seems to change and we find ourselves somewhat agitated or frustrated. We puzzle at where this sense of unsettle has come from since we were quite content only a short time earlier.

This is the subconscious 'ripple effect'. What others emit around us, we unintentionally absorb. Unless we are cognizant of it and make a conscious effort to prevent it, we find ourselves emotionally in sync with another, positively or negatively.

Think also of times when you have been in an irritated frame of mind and have encountered someone incredibly light-hearted and positive. Somehow you seem to feel better about yourself, the negativity lifts and a spirit of contentedness seems to prevail. We find ourselves drawn to those who emit this positive mindset and avoid those who are negative and emotionally draining to us.

Our environment can also play a significant role in our overall mindset. Many years ago I was asked to do a mass hire for a billion-dollar organization. The owners were Oriental and believed in transparency. Every employee worked in one large, expansive room. The President's and Executive's desks were in the middle of this room with the employees' desks encircling them.

All meeting rooms around the outside of the room faced into the center and all meeting rooms had clear glass frontages and doors. At any given time all could see what was going on in these rooms.

There were no cubicles or dividers of any form, not even Human Resources; simply flat desks placed at angles to one another so no two desks faced each other minimizing conversations.

Although the company was incredibly successful, the rate of absenteeism and turnover was excessively high.

I myself found working in this environment particularly difficult as there was no buffer of any kind to block the flow of energies circulating around the room.

Many staff felt this unexplainable need to go walking at lunchtime or sit in their cars and doze as they had trouble staying awake through the afternoon. Numerous mentioned to me the need to drive with their windows partially open (even in inclement weather) to stay awake during their commute home. Once they got home, they needed a brief nap to 'kick start' themselves again.

The company was very progressive, the management very good and fair. However the ripple effect and sensory overload of so much free-flowing energy was debilitating to many.

The reason I share this particular story is to emphasize that it isn't just the energy emitted from any one person that we need to recognize. The energies in our overall environment emit a collective ripple effect. Interestingly when the majority of employees were excited or inspired by something the company was doing the revenues spiked significantly. When employees were bored, uninspired or demotivated revenues dropped drastically and absenteeism rose.

We thrive on each other's positivity and contentedness and deteriorate with the opposite around us.

We also forget about the 'ripple effect' of timelines. How often have you set your sights on something and found you're in that wonderful 'hurry up and wait' holding pattern. Frustrating as it may be, we disregard the fact that others directly or indirectly participate in our decision-making timelines.

You may want that perfect house now but the person who owns it isn't ready to put it on the market yet. You may want that wonderful new position but if the present employee still holds that job, you will have to wait until they move along and vacate that role. You have been longing to find that perfect partner, but they may still be going through the struggles of pre-breakup or recovery from terminating a relationship and not quite ready for you yet.

We're aware of the sandbox we reside in but don't usually consider other sandboxes and the goals, dreams, wishes and timelines of those occupants. True synchronicity occurs when timelines, goals and dreams for all concerned come together in unison.

When something better is in the wings we may actually be delayed through circumstances so we can be accommodated. These delays happen at an energy level and if we have focused patience, allowing this process to flow and unfold as intended, we reap the benefits.

A woman going through a difficult separation confided to me that she had found the perfect house for her and her children. Unfortunately the house already had a conditional offer on it but she was determined to bump the current offer. I mentioned to her that bumping would not be in her best interest energetically and if the house was meant to be hers it would come to her regardless without negatively displacing another. She was impatient and insisted she was presenting an offer that afternoon.

I asked her to delay a day with her offer, drive down the street and around the corner to see if any other properties were for sale. She argued. I asked her to humour me and take the time to look.

She finally agreed to wait until the following morning to bump these other purchasers. Prior to meeting her agent at the house at 11:00 a.m. she reluctantly drove further down the street as I had asked.

Coincidentally (not), a new For Sale sign was just being placed on a property about five doors away. She loved the look of this newly listed house and the lot but thought it was probably just that bit out of her price range.

Regardless, she called her agent and asked if she could see this new property first before writing up the offer on 'her' house. As fate would have it, not only did this newly listed house have significantly more features, larger property, was totally renovated and move in ready, but was also thirty thousand dollars less.

Immediately after viewing, her agent drew up the offer on the newly listed property, it was accepted without sign back and she happily moved in thirty days later.

Had she forced her offer the day before in an attempt to bump those other purchasers, they may not have been able to firm up. She would have been committed to follow through with her original offer on the house she 'just had to' buy. The purchasers whose offer she would have bumped would probably have placed an offer on the newly listed property five doors down instead.

Her negative actions would likely have resulted in her acquiring the house she just had to have at all costs (for thirty-thousand dollars more). The other buyers would have reaped the rewards of the much better purchase for a lesser price instead of her. By considering another ahead of herself she opened up the opportunity to trust that something better was in the offing for her. That is exactly what happened.

* * *

This is how God, Karma, Universe, Synchronicity, Energies and Ripple Effect works in our favour if we trust it and use it. Allow the power of your own energies to blend with the powers around us to produce the end result you desire.

STEP 6

YOUR WORLD
Don't make someone else's world yours and don't allow someone to make you his or her world. Be PART of their world and let them be PART of yours.

We come into this world on our own. We are meant to walk our own path in conjunction with others until we take our final breath and depart on our own. Somehow in the process called relationships we seem to lose our independence, our personal route, and ourselves.

To accommodate those we care about we happily compromise and blend their ideals with ours. Sometimes these compromises end up being a better fit for us so we adopt these new methods, values, or beliefs. Often though, we struggle to find that balance between the shared path and the individual one. This is when newly empty nester parents struggle. It is also when new relationships and newlyweds move from that 'honeymoon' stage of the relationship to finding a daily routine.

If we think singularly within the structure of a partnership we can maintain that healthy balance that so many of us lose.

Thinking singularly does not mean thinking only of yourself or pretending that you're single. It means moving ahead with your life and path while others walk theirs. Rather than one blended path being walked by both, you have two separate paths of life being lived simultaneously in the comfortable framework of a relationship. It means not shelving your goals and dreams so someone else can fulfill theirs. Rather, finding that happy median where both can pursue their goals and dreams in unison, unless one party is wholeheartedly happy to step back and help the other pursue their goals.

Several years ago I spoke with a young man who had been devastated by the departure of his partner. They had met during their first year at university and moved in together shortly thereafter. With no financial assistance, including for their education, she suggested he work full-time and support her while she obtained her Bachelor's Degree. Once she graduated they could reverse roles, he could return to school full-time and she would support him. He agreed.

Her B.A. turned into a Masters and then a PhD. At times he needed to work two jobs to make ends meet, but throughout it all he supported her both emotionally and financially. She continually promised once she graduated she would acquire a well-paying job and their roles would reverse.

After seven long years of waiting the end was in sight for him. She was set to graduate in April and he eagerly anticipated returning to school in September to continue his educational journey.

Ten days after graduating she secured an extremely lucrative job close to home. He was ecstatic. Then she dropped the bomb.

She stated that during her final year of studies she began feeling differently about their relationship and now that her education was complete, decided it would be best if she pursued her new career and her life on her own.

To say he was both blindsided and devastated would be an understatement. He had literally put his life on hold for her for seven years and supported her while she followed her dream – to the tune of approximately one hundred thousand dollars.

She was not prepared to fulfill her part of the arrangement leaving him feeling hurt, used, and nearly broke.

Now on his own he financially couldn't leave work to return to school full-time so earned his degree through part-time studies. As you can imagine, it took him considerably longer to graduate. However through this long arduous process he never lost sight of his own career goals and dreams.

Looking back he realized had they positioned themselves differently they both could have gone to school full-time and worked part-time to financially accommodate both dreams simultaneously.

Had they not met and both been single they would have arranged individual finances, housing, expenses, etc. based on single needs. Although they blended into a relationship they should have kept the singular process and walked their individual paths to reach their individual goals.

Another young woman I spoke to faced similar circumstances when a man she was seriously dating (although only after a short amount of time) suggested a similar situation, but roles reversed. He suggested she pursue her education while he temporarily shelved his. He would work to support her until he could get into school, which would be at least another year, and then he would continue with his degree.

"I don't want someone else putting their life on hold for me," she confided to me.

"If he wants to finish his degree he should, that shouldn't have anything to do with me," she rationalized it further.

"Also, what if the relationship doesn't last? He'll have forfeited three or four years of his life doing something that he doesn't want to do for me. That isn't right."

This along with a few other issues brought the relationship to an end and he reverted to his original educational plans.

Think of yourself as a seed and how you will grow. If you plant one seed on its' own and nurture it, it will grow quickly and blossom. If you take two seeds and plant them side by side, given the proper space, they will both grow into beautiful healthy plants just as the individual seed did. If you take one seed and plant it directly on top of the other in the soil, one of two things will happen. Either the lower plant will try to grow through the upper plant, pushing it out or causing it to break apart, or find some way to grow around the upper plant. Even by growing around the upper seed, the lower seeds' stem will be bent and deformed.

The upper plant, unless too badly damaged by the lower plants' growth, will grow but will also be stunted, as its root system will be stifled by the lower plant.

Should both plants manage to grow in spite of each other, the growth for both will be restricted because of the smothering proximity of the other.

Think of you, the seed, in relation to the other seeds in your life. If given enough space, caring, and nurturing, all seeds will grow successfully. Improperly planted without sufficient room to grow, all plants will suffer in some form; some forfeiting their growth or even existence at the expense of another.

Throughout your life always think of yourself as the seed, which needs to be nurtured first and foremost by you, then by those around you. Be aware of the other seeds 'in your pot' and how you want to nurture and support them also.

Allow yourself to grow as you need to. Give yourself the space and independence to do so. Make your world co-exist effectively with those around you and vice versa. Trust that by doing this while still holding true to yourself in the process, all can grow and blossom as intended. Those who can't, won't or don't want to for whatever reason should be 'transplanted' elsewhere.

Embrace, love and respect your World for it is yours alone to share as you choose. Contentedly enjoy and support the Worlds of those around you for what they offer you and vice versa. Allow Worlds to revolve in harmony where possible, but never sacrifice your World for another's.

Imagine your own world, your life, as a tangible object to be cared for, nurtured and filled with all that inspires you. It is yours to love. Just as our daughter wanted to travel to France when she was twelve and Costa Rica at the age of fourteen, her next inspiration became Asia once she finished University. She set her vision on it.

With her destination clearly in mind she set her budget, rough timeline for the trip, earned the funds needed, then set off. We were not sure how long she would be gone, neither was she; all depended on how far her money took her. She covered Thailand, Vietnam, India and Indonesia over a three-month period. When her funds ran out she headed home.

She returned to work but after a short period felt she needed yet another temporary change of venue in some way. She put out the general thought of change and allowed the opportunity to present itself. Within two weeks, through a chance reconnection with a former employer, she had an offer to go to California for several months.

Apprehensively she approached her present employer about another leave of absence. Fearing her employer would be furious, possibly even fire her, she was stunned when he seemed overjoyed and asked how soon she wanted to leave.

Unbeknownst to her, rapid expansion and delays in construction timelines had put her employer into a position of temporary overstaffing. He had been panicking as to how he was going to give all of his staff the hours they expected and needed.

Our daughter's request for short-term leave was a blessing in disguise for her employer. She departed for California a week later. Interestingly her return coincided exactly with the completion of the expansion and need for full staff again.

Returning from California she once again immersed herself in work and saving.

This time her sights were set on a shift in career path by returning to school for her second degree.

Before she could talk to her employer about her career thoughts, he offered her a position in exactly the field she had envisioned herself doing once her education was finished.

She happily accepted the new role with part-time hours to accommodate her education. She followed the stepping stones needed to fulfill her current dream by enrolling into a two-year program that would give her the formal skillsets she wanted for her future endeavors.

In order to accommodate her class schedule she felt she needed to move to the city. With only weeks until school commenced she began to panic. Every feasible unit was being snapped up, many before she even had a chance to see them.

I asked her to stop worrying and focus as she usually does. Within twenty-four hours she saw a unit, which had just become available in an ideal location. It was considerably larger than anything she had actually been able to see before losing out to other renters.

Contentedly ensconced in her city unit and with one year of her two-year program behind her, the demands of her part-time job, her employers' need for more hours from her and distance between work and home were becoming increasingly difficult. In fairness to her employer, who now needed someone onsite full time, she terminated her employment and sought a position in her chosen field closer to home.

As with everything else Kendra has done, she put her thoughts and dreams and ultimate goal out with her conversations and actions. Within weeks she was told of an opening that was less than what she was qualified for but could eventually open the door for the actual position she envisioned herself holding. She was offered and accepted the more entry level position with the intent of moving up as openings came available.

The company was expanding rapidly. Through her eagerness to gain knowledge about the organization and her team player attitude, she caught the attention of the Executives. They quickly learned of Kendra's experience and background from her resume and saw the potential in her.

As synchronicity works in our favour if we allow it, those doors of opportunity for advancement opened up and she was promoted three times in a six-week period into the very position she was going to school for. Many would say she was just at the right place at the right time. Absolutely! That is how our envisioning in relation to synchronicity works. By accepting the opportunity presented to her, then the stepping stones to her ultimate goal *and taking action* to create her reality Kendra attained the role she sought. She intentionally defined and created her World

Define clearly and only the exact outcome you want and how you envision your world. Put your effort into it with your actions while being considerate of those around you. Take the opportunities when and as they present themselves and allow the power of synchronicity to lend a hand as it always will if you hold true to yourself and your dreams. Cherish and treat your World and your life as a possession for it truly is yours and yours alone. Happily share your World and your life with others and savour what they have to offer in return.

OUR GROUNDWORK & FOUNDATION

(WHERE DOES IT ALL BEGIN?)

From infancy we are taught to take baby steps and be cautious. We are told to 'watch where we're going and what we are doing'. We are led to believe it can't work if it isn't complicated. We are constantly guided and instructed on what we can and can't do. Unintentionally others set limitations for us in an attempt to keep us out of harms' way. We then add to our list of limitations through our fears and apprehensions around succeeding and failing.

If we take a different approach to our lives in general and how we accomplish things, we may discover that often the simplest most direct route from A to B creates the greatest results.

The basic concepts in this book give a refreshing way of dealing with ourselves first and foremost and the simplest route from A to B. We can accept that it is ok and even necessary to be selfish some of the time because in the big scheme of things it is ultimately beneficial to others as well.

I have seen my daughter apply these fundamentals time and again to achieve the results she wants. She displays what I refer to as 'quiet determination'. She doesn't need to discuss her thoughts with others and obtain their opinions and ideas. She just sets about doing what she sets her mind to.

When our daughter was in Grade 2 the teacher asked if anyone would volunteer to introduce their class during the upcoming Variety Show. According to the teacher our daughter's hand went up instantly. As a matter of fact her hand was the only one up initially. Slowly several others raised their hands also. The teacher pointed out that it meant speaking on stage in front of classmates as well as teachers and parents. Several raised hands came down. The teacher continued to explain that there would probably be about three hundred and fifty in the audience. The rest of the hands dropped except our daughter's. The teacher lovingly said to our daughter, "you sure you want to do this honey?' Our daughter simply nodded.

She was given the task of writing out what she wanted to say to the audience, review it with her teacher and be responsible for delivering the message at all three shows.

When she told us what she had volunteered for, we were pleasantly surprised as she did have a bit of a shy side sometimes. I asked her what made her put her hand up. She said it scared her so she thought she should get over it.

Why can a seven-year-old take the bull by the horns so to speak yet we adults are left quaking in our boots and back away from anything that remotely unsettles us. It is called conditioning and overcomplicating.

Take the simple approach, be consistent and be generous with your thoughts, feelings, ideas, humour and love to others. Give financially to those less fortunate, even if only a small amount is all you can give. It truly is the thought that counts.

Say 'no' when necessary. You will inadvertently be doing someone else a favour in the process.

Show your individuality. If you mirror another everyone will see it and know it isn't the true you. They will feel you are 'hiding' from them in some way.

BUT...WHAT IF YOU FEEL LIKE THE LOST SOUL?

So often I work with teens and adults alike who truly feel like lost souls. They are unsure of their natural gifts, talents and abilities often because they have never had an opportunity to tap into them. Their natural aptitudes lay dormant like a gold mine yet to be discovered.

More often than not these individuals constantly display their unfound talents through their very words or actions, but because these abilities come to them so naturally they are automatically dismissed.

Let me share the example of forty-two year old Yvonne. During our hour-long session she continuously expressed her frustration around her direction in life. She was unhappy in her present position yet didn't know what she could do that would generate an income and be more fulfilling. She also stated countless times about how she loved to write, journal, share ideas with others, make lists, and document – about anything and everything it seemed. Finally she took a breath at which point I said to her "do you realize over the last hour you have been answering your own question again and again?"

She fell silent for a minute, then quietly replied, "no I haven't."

"Absolutely. For the last hour you have repeatedly stated how much you love to write, how passionate you are about it, how you can sit and write for hours and how you have several story lines already clearly defined in your mind," I said.

"Oh, but you could never make a living at it! My parents told me from the time I was little that it would be a good pastime but you need to get a real job and earn a real living, otherwise you could starve as a writer!"

I could actually hear the fear in her voice with her last statement.

I asked if she had ever entered any of her works it in a writing contest to which she replied no because she might be rejected. I asked her if she had ever considered a career such as ghost writing, freelancing for the local paper or magazines, becoming a journalist, speech writer or media assistant.

Her eyes misted as she nodded. Although her high school English teacher had strongly encouraged her to pursue a journalism career and it was her dream throughout her teens, her parents' words rang so clearly in her ears that she altered her path completely and chose a mainstream job. Her parents were elated while she was quietly despondent but resigned to the career choice that suited them.

Now years later she still struggled with recognizing and using her true natural gifts and abilities because those very abilities, which could have led her into a successfully happy career path, were deemed worthless and quelled completely.

Interestingly, immediately after our session Yvonne enrolled in an online University level journalism and creative writing course. She now earns an extremely nice living as a freelance writer.

Our teens seem to struggle the most though. Our school system conditions our youth to believe they need to know what they want to be and do with their lives by the tender age of thirteen or fourteen. They stress over choosing the right courses to ensure they don't make a mistake and often in the process 'freeze' their decision-making out of fear.

Just like the young man who applied for the clerk's position and ended up with an amazing career, action of any kind will produce a result that will in some form move your life forward. Your actions may not seem important initially but even the simplest actions generate energy which creates opportunities of some form. For every action there is a reaction – yes I have said that before.

Think of yourself sitting behind the wheel of your car parked in your driveway. Unsure of where you're headed or even which way to go, you just remain parked. As long as you stay in this parked mode whether for a minute, an hour, a day, a week or an eternity, nothing significant in your life will happen. You will just remain parked.

However, if you turn the key, start the car and pull out of the driveway, you have taken action to create a reaction of some form. Even if you don't know where you are going you will end up somewhere. Sometimes it is just that simple process of starting an action with a 'what if' attitude that leads to something or somewhere significant. You would never know or ever have the experience if you don't start the whole process by taking action, turning your ignition on and starting out.

If you feel you are heading in the wrong direction, simply change your route. This is the control every individual has over their own lives. If you don't like where you're heading change your course but for the very least venture forth and see where that road and course may lead you. It could be somewhere very profound. You will never know unless you go.

...IT ALL BEGINS WITH...OUR NATURAL TRAITS

From the earliest age what interests and excites our child through play can signal their fundamental natural career path in adulthood.

A child who loves building and making things should consider building in some form as an adult. 'Building' can range from computers to automobiles, architecture to a space arm. A child who constantly plays at being a doctor, nurse or vet, should go into a nurturing caregiving career of some form. A child who loves to pretend he/she is a teacher should seek a career in a teaching capacity. Children who love spending hours drawing or painting should seek an artistic field. Those who happily spent hours with a musical instrument...you get the picture.

I had a conversation with a young seventeen-year-old who told me she was going to University in the fall and pursuing a career in journalism. Her tone was less than passionate. She actually seemed despondent as she spoke. I felt she was a very creative individual but in a very different way; she had an amazing talent to design and sew. She stated that since the age of twelve not only had she been designing and sewing clothes for herself and her mother but had also been making bridesmaids dresses, wedding gowns and even her father's suits.

Her eyes lit up and she absolutely glowed as she talked about her 'seamstress hobby.' I asked her why she wasn't pursuing a career in this field as she was clearly passionate about it. She explained that her family thought it was a wonderful pastime and hobby but she needed to have a degree more mainstream. Hence she picked journalism because she thought it would be relatively easy for her and appease her family at the same time.

I suggested she talk to her parents, get her university deposit back, approach a fashion design school or college program and pursue what she so clearly loved. With only six weeks until the new school term in September and all classes full she pulled together a portfolio regardless and approached the most highly recognized college about entering their fashion program. This is where most would have halted and resigned themselves to either delay until the following year or shelving their dream altogether. She persevered.

The institute was so impressed with her prior accomplishments they created a spot in the September class for her. After completing only her first year, she was voted most likely to be the countries' next 'up and coming' top designer. Her career began to flourish long before she graduated from her program.

****

Unfortunately this is where so many of our youth are confused, frustrated and discouraged just as this young seventeen year old initially was. They are given guidance and direction contrary to what they should really be doing based on their fundamental abilities and interests. They dismiss their 'natural calling' and replace it with perceived goals.

How do we as parents and teachers promote this self-awareness and positive mindset in our youth from the earliest age?

Always make your message to your children simple and direct. Help them embrace these simple ideals:

- Be who you need to be, not what other people want you to be. *(Step 3 - Individuality)*

- Do not be afraid to take the leap, there are no mistakes only experiences.
  (Step 4 - Goal & Vision / Step 5 - Ripple Effect Congruency & Synchronicity / Step 6 - Your World)

- Circumstances don't matter, only your state of mind matters, in other words only you decide how to react to them.
  (Step 1 - Generosity / Step 2 - Balance)

- There are no coincidences in life, everything is for a reason so go with the flow, don't resist it, if you go with it, it will always take you were you need to be.
  (Step 5 - Ripple Effect Congruency & Synchronicity)

- Love yourself, act on your highest excitement.
  (Step 2 - Balance / Step 3 - Individuality)

- You don't need to go out of yourself to find answers, everything you need to know is inner self.
  (Step 1 - Generosity / Step 3 - Individuality / Step 6 - Your World)

- Perception is not real it is only an illusion so don't perceive and don't let anybody measure you by their perception, for they don't know you.
  (Step 3 - Individuality)

- Embrace life, for life embraces you.
  (Step 4 - Goal & Vision / Step 5 - Ripple Effect Congruency & Synchronicity)

- Don't resist your natural self, act upon your highest excitement, you are unique, challenge your limits and do what you love to do.
  (Step 3 - Individuality)

AS A PARENT:

- ✓ Have no expectations so there is no pressure to perform. This allows your children to make their own reality according to what they are interested in.
  (Step 3 - Individuality)

- ✓ Only guide them, suggest and give as much support as they let you give.
  (Step 1 - Generosity / Step 2 – Balance / Step 6 - Your World)

- ✓ The rest is up to them. Respect their right to individualism.
  (Step 3 - Individuality /Step 4 - Goal & Vision / Step 5 - Ripple Effect Congruency & Synchronicity)

Youth is the most exciting time in ones' life, there is an appetite for adventure, for life, a sense of justice and a moral innocence. At the same time our youth desperately subject themselves to this perceived invisible rule, which says: you need to project yourself a certain way to be able to fit, act in a certain way to be accepted by society.

Unfortunately when that happens, they become afraid to act naturally, because society makes them believe they have no other choice but to pretend and that becomes detrimental to their mental and physical health.

The role of social media has a huge impact and has created a great deal of pressure on youth in particular to conform.

THE GOLDEN RULE:

Regardless of age, don't resist your natural self. Act upon your highest excitement, you are unique, challenge your limits and do what you love to do.

...AND ONE OTHER THING...

One other element that is highly relevant to growth and development: Everybody is creative but when you have a chance to be in different environments through travel and change, the creativity becomes more profound.

The interaction and the ability to understand more about cultures and traditions, becomes essential, a part of you, without even trying, and that brings participation into action, whatever that is.

More important is the human connection, the understanding (not the perception) of the behind the scenes, why and how a society acts, not to judge and condemn, but to love and appreciate our differences.

When you are exposed to different dynamics of any kind, inevitably your horizons broaden just through exposure and experience. What once may have seemed significant often becomes irrelevant with newfound knowledge and awareness.

Why bring the dynamics of youth into the equation? If we can give children the means to be confident in themselves and trusting of their own abilities and judgement at a very early age, they will automatically apply the aforementioned way and means of fulfilling their goals and dreams without needing to 'learn' it.

It will become instinctual to them as they step forward fearlessly.

Regardless of age, culture, nationality or beliefs, effectively use your Mind, Set your sights definitively, and Go with passion and excitement.

THE EASIER PATH TO SUCCESS & GENUINE HAPPINESS

Ways to Incorporate 'The Six Steps' & Shift Your Mind Set, To GO!

- Think only of the end result of what you want and fall in love with it in your mind…create physical action around it (phone calls, networking, education, etc. to bring it to fruition. Create Action Around It!
  (Step 4 - Goal & Vision, Step 5 - Ripple Effect Congruency & Synchronicity)

- *Don't* envision the winning lottery ticket; **DO** envision the lifestyle you enjoy living *as a result of* that winning ticket or wealth coming in some form (that money may come in a different form than what you envision but come it will).
  (Step 2 - Balance)

- *Don't* envision a successful job interview; **DO** envision only the outcome - happily and successfully already in that position. Assume from the beginning it is already yours and state that to yourself.
  (STEP 6 - Your World)

- *Don't* envision a particular man/woman coming into your life to make you happy; **DO** envision living with a wonderful person in a solid contented relationship/

marriage. If you are happy in yourself first and foremost you will both find your way to each other to create an amazing relationship.
(Step 5 - Ripple Effect Congruency & Synchronicity, Step 6 – Your World)

- **DO** trust that your decisions will have an ultimate positive ripple effect on all.
(Step 1 - Balance / Step 5 - Ripple Effect Congruency & Synchronicity)

- **DO** trust also that the opportunity and result you seek will materialize in the timeframe most appropriate.
(Step 5 - Ripple Effect Congruency & Synchronicity)

- **DO TAKE the opportunity immediately when it does come!**
(Step 4 - Goal & Vision / Step 5 - Ripple Effect Congruency & Synchronicity)

- **DO Respect and appreciate all you have here and now.**
(Step 1 - Generosity / Step 3 - Individuality)

- **DO Be Content in yourself** for who and what you are at this point in time. Be you as only you can be as there is no one else on the planet quite like you. Embrace this!
(Step 3 - Individuality)

- **DO** Focus on sharing your contentedness with those around you.
(Step 1- Generosity)

- **DO** Allow and encourage others to follow their individual dreams but regardless of what life throws at you, always hold true to yourself!
  (Step 1 - Generosity / Step 3 - Individuality / Step 6 - Your World)

- **Lastly, trust yourself**, set your sights, live every dream you have throughout your life but always savour what you have here and now. For no matter what stage, phase or position you have in life at present, you are special in your own right and can direct your World and your life any way you choose. **<u>Be content.</u>**
  (Step 2 - Balance / Step 3 - Individuality / Step 6 - Your World)

Our greatest empowerment and path to success and genuine happiness lies in our ability to interact effectively with others while holding true to ourselves. Always respect yourself as an individual, define your own benchmarks and treat others in kind as you expect to be treated.

The six steps are not singular, they are linked and flow together to create the final overall result; your life as you want it to be. These simplest of thoughts and actions create that positive energy and vibration in and around us that is unimaginably powerful, positive, measurably successful and sustainable. It is total congruency and synchronicity in ourselves and our world.

Embrace this new mindset to view beyond the physical body. Understand and adopt these concepts to incorporate your inner power with the power of energy, congruency and synchronicity to more easily create the outcome you desire. Stop *trying* to make your life work. That mindset does truly turn your life *into* work. Instead, enjoy what each day and everything has to offer in its simplest form.

When we are totally congruent and positive in ourselves and our life, we will discover we are also empowering those around us through our very presence. By also intentionally incorporating others in our positive intent we empower ourselves in the process through sheer ripple effect.

Act on your thoughts and ideas to make your mark and leave your footprint every day and accept full responsibility for your decisions and actions.

Live your life to the fullest since it is yours alone and only you can truly determine your fate. Do not be fearful of what lies ahead. View your life as the great adventure, find your excitement, seek what inspires you, set you mind and go with passion, caring and understanding of yourself and all around you.

AND FINALLY...TAKE ACTION...

...Every day live these simple six steps...

_____

STEP 1 - GENEROSITY
Start with...a kind word, gesture, smile...some donation of kindness to yourself & others

_____

STEP 2 – BALANCE
Trust your decisions...say 'no' when necessary to maintain balance for yourself

_____

STEP 3 – INDIVIDUALITY
Be yourself! You'll be surprised at how many will love you for who you really are!

_____

STEP 4 - GOAL & VISION
Set your 'want'... be prepared to act on it as it will come very quickly...

_____

STEP 5 - RIPPLE EFFECT CONGRUENCY & SYNCHRONICITY
Trust your 'want' will come when and as it should for the good of all

_____

STEP 6 - YOUR WORLD
Live your own life...expect and allow others to do the same

_____

MIND SET, GO!
Think it...Love it...Live it!

About The Author, Books, Programs And Services

SPEAKING ENGAGEMENTS:

Deborah is a widely sought after Key Note Speaker. Depending on your venue Deborah's topics can cover but are not limited to...

- Trait Reading Others Effectively Personally & Professionally
- Mind Set, Go – Creating Your Reality
- Communication & Inter-personal Relationships
- Health and Wellness
- Understanding & Relating To Our Youth More Effectively
- Mediumship and Reaching Out to Those We Have Lost

...all from a refreshingly new energy-based perspective.

Each speaking engagement can be customized to suit your needs, from a 30 or 60 minute Key Note Presentation at your AGM to a two-day Workshop intensive for your staff or group.

Deborah's books in her Series 'The Deborah Johnson Series' available for purchase:

*NEW	-	**TRAIT READER**
*NEW	-	**MIND SET, GO!**
*AWARD WINNING	-	**DISCOVER THE MAGIC**
*HEALTH & WELLNESS	-	**LOOK WITHIN, HEAL WITHOUT**

ABOUT:

TRAIT READER: *Beyond* Body Language...discover three *new* Levels of perception that you can benefit from in your Business and Personal life. Learn how to accurately identify the base traits of a person or situation within 10 seconds. Use this knowledge to enrich your relationships, decisions, understanding and awareness of others and even yourself.

TRAIT READER TRAINING PROGRAM:

If you are interested in developing your Trait Reading skills to a greater degree please email Deborah at deborah@deborahjohnson.ca for information about her Beginner, Intermediate and Master Level training programs.

MIND SET, GO!: Discover the KIS Principle of Fulfilling Your Life, Fulfilling Your Goals, Fulfilling Your Dreams with such a Simple Straight-forward Mindset, anyone can successfully adopt it and reap the benefits.

DISCOVER THE MAGIC: Three-time International Award Winning 'Discover the Magic' received International recognition in the Los Angeles International Book Awards winning in 'New Age Non-Fiction' and 'Social Change' categories. Discover the Magic was also named one of the best reads of 2011 by 'USA Best Books of 2011'. Discover the Magic gives you the knowledge and tools to understand yourself better and communicate with others more effectively.

LOOK WITHIN, HEAL WITHOUT: Look Within, Heal Without is an Exercise/ Metaphysical Awareness book and stretching program. Through 20 minutes a day of simple physical stretching and breathing coupled with an understanding of how our emotions contribute to our overall wellness, we can regain greater control over own health and well-being. Testimonials state that this easy routine has proven to be incredibly successful with weight loss, lowering blood pressure, even improving one's golf game significantly!

Available by emailing deborah@deborahjohnson.ca, or wherever paperbacks are sold.

**PRIVATE
SESSIONS:**

All of Deborah's sessions are either ½ hour or 1 hour in length and are done by phone or skype. This mode of communicating allows Deborah clients to be able to reach her from anywhere in the world and benefit from her services. To arrange an individual session: email deborah@deborahjohnson.ca. or call 705 725-1090.

BIOGRAPHY

Author and Keynote Speaker, Deborah Johnson is an Internationally-known personal and corporate Visionary, Medium, and Inspirational Motivator focused on Esteem and Empowerment. Deborah utilizes over 20 years' experience to coach, instruct and direct others to move past their blocks and achieve their full potential.

Deborah works with clients from all walks seeking guidance and direction in their lives. She also works extensively with corporate clients offering an esteem and empowerment based venue which dovetails effectively with traditional business practices.

A well-known TV and radio personality who has been featured in numerous books and magazines, Deborah brings her enthusiasm, integrity and extensive knowledge to her clients as she invites, inspires, and motivates her diverse client base to strive beyond the limitations they have set for themselves.

Deborah's newly-released 2-Book Series and related Programs 'Trait Reader' and 'Mind, Set, Go!' gives the reader two new venues of awareness. Her previous 2 books 'Discover The Magic' and 'Look Within, Heal Without' are also available for added insight.

Through her workshops and seminars Deborah trains and coaches individuals and groups to recognize and enhance their innate gifts while her skills and inspirational messages make Deborah a widely sought after Keynote Speaker.

You may contact Deborah Johnson at:
www.deborahjohnson.ca
deborah@deborahjohnson.ca

Biography

Kendra Johnson

 After graduating from the University of Guelph with an Honours Marketing Degree, Kendra took 3 months off to travel Southeast Asia. Along with these travels, she developed her hobby for literature through journaling and blog posts. With travel as a passion, she jet set again shortly after returning home for another 2-month stint in California. While she is still passionate about writing and travel, she now resides in Toronto with her Great Dane, Merlin, and works in Events, specifically in the Hospitality industry.

Printed in the United States
By Bookmasters